CW01095894

The Rebuild

Stuart Cooper

Stuart "Coopsie" Cooper

WRITERS' CHAMPION

Published by MA Publishing (Penzance)
Email: mapublisher@yahoo.com, www.mapublisher.org.uk
Released on May 2023

Printed in the UK,

ISBN-13: 978-1-910499-99-3

Cover designed by Mayar Akash
Cover image: by Suzanne Phillips
Typeset in Times Roman

Paper printed on is FSC Certified, lead free, acid free, buffered paper made from wood-based pulp. Our paper meets the ISO 9706 standard for permanent paper. As such, paper will last several hundred years when stored.

Dedication

I am dedicating this to the unbelievably brave fire-crews, from Penzance, St Ives & Hayle, Cornwall.

They somehow kept me alive long enough for the Ambulance crew to arrive.

The phenomenal 'Angels' in the Welsh Hospital that saved a life that wasn't supposed to be saved.

Surgeons who went above and beyond any duty of care.

The Intensive Care Unit that I was in it will stay with me until the day I die.

Nurses

Physiotherapist

Occupational Therapists.

Psychology departments who literally rebuilt a person from scratch. Pushing me to surpass limits I never realised I had.

A genuinely World Class medical facility in Wales is, quite literally, the only reason I am able to type these words. If it wasn't for them, there would be no me!

To everyone in that stunning hospital, I say THANK YOU!

Acknowledgements

I would like acknowledge Morriston Hospital and their amazing staff.

Suzanne Phillips for her time, energy and her lovely artwork that I have used as the cover image, and for her permission to use it.

Mayar Akash for championing me and publishing my work through his "Writers' Champion" label.

Thank you to Helen Owen for taking the photos and Daniel Owen for transporting the artwork to the hospital ward.

My heart, mind and soul is thankful and full of gratitude for so many people at so many stages of my life and recovery who have helped and supported me; who I am acknowledging here by name, please forgive me if I can't remember surnames.

Peter Drew	Louise
Jeremy Yarrow	Nic
Helen Watkins	Jane
Jo Bowes	Louise (Sister)
Sid	Hannah
Sophie Limbert	Jo
Louise Denieffe	Siobhan
Janine Evans	Emma
Claire Poole	Donna
Menna Davies	Tash
Laura	Laura
Grace	Hannah
Carys	Jane
Keith	Linda
Linda	Claire
Shauna	

CONTENT

Introduction

What you are about to read, is not a story, as such!

You are going to be taken on "The Journey" of a man who, in October 2019 had his life changed forever.

A man who went to bed in Cornwall, after his usual 16 hour working day, and was woken by being engulfed in what can only be described as "an inferno!".

You'll read about how he somehow managed to get out, walk to his neighbour, get them out of bed by banging their door. This is despite having 66% 3rd and 4th degree burns, and NOBODY, not even the firemen can understand how I got out.

You'll find out how, after the firemen showed up, this man who was obliterated by the inferno woke up from a coma 2 months later, in Wales. Waking to a world that was incomparable to the one that existed before his accident. Not only because he had lost the ability to do ANYTHING, even talk or walk. But also because this new world was full of something called "Corona Virus" and everyone was wearing masks.

What had happened to the world in my absence? Apart from my children being told that, in all likeliness their dad isn't going to survive. I'll never know!

But, through the power of poetry, and a little explaining between each passage, You're going to discover the existence I've been rebuilt to lead. I cannot, and will not call it "a life". Life is for living, I don't get to live. I get to exist!

Locked away 7 days per week, just so that my destroyed shell can't be judged by society. I simply exist, locked away until I'm called to hospital for my next excruciating round of surgery. That is my world, all I have to look forward to.

But, to me, it's imperative that I tell the world about "The Angels" that not only saved my life, but rebuilt a person from nothing. These people are the most amazing people I've ever come across, and they should be given all the recognition they deserve. Even if they simply say, "We were just doing our job". They weren't! They went above and beyond a duty of care. I simply HAVE TO shout this from the rooftops, to anyone willing to listen.

You are about to be introduced to these people.

You are about to read about how special they are.

You are about to read about a darkness I wouldn't wish upon anyone.
You will read the odd bit of swearing. But it's difficult to be truthful without simply saying exactly how I feel.

There will be bits that make you laugh, cry, maybe even get angry. You're reading honesty in its purest form.

This "Journey" is going to have the odd, very random twist. Some topics will make you think, "What the heck is he on about?"

If it was a simple journey, it would be a boring read. However, thanks to those Angels in Wales giving me "homework" while I was under their care for 9 months, things go from angelic to manic very quickly.

Fear not. All will become clear as I talk you through three years of dancing with the Devil, cheating Death himself, and finding his release in the form of the written word!

Seems almost perverse to say, I hope you enjoy the journey I'm about to take you on. But I truly hope you do, because I can assure you. I most certainly have not!

So, allow me to firstly introduce you to Stuart Cooper, AKA "Coopsie". The person who, in his mind went from being a man, to become a monster!

THE MAN

A simple, loving and caring soul.
For others, he did live.
Himself, well he had nothing.
His life was just a sieve!

All good taken from his life.
Through no fault of his own.
His marriage ended suddenly.
Kids gone, he was alone!

He'll admit this hit him harder.
Than anything had before.
He attempted the most selfish act.
He couldn't face life anymore.

His world had become empty.
Unfortunately he'd fail.
After concocting a little recipe.
A vodka and tablet cocktail.

He took enough tablets.
To kill off a small tribe.
The sadness he felt within.
Impossible to describe.

Of course, because it's Coopsie.
As he took his tablets weeping.
The only thing that happened.
Was him spending 8 hours sleeping.

He woke up feeling guilty.
And even to this day.
Can't make sense of his first action.
He'd phone his ex to say.

Last night I tried a selfish act.
Something no parent should do.
I tried, but failed to end my life.
Because I've lost my kids and you.

cont.

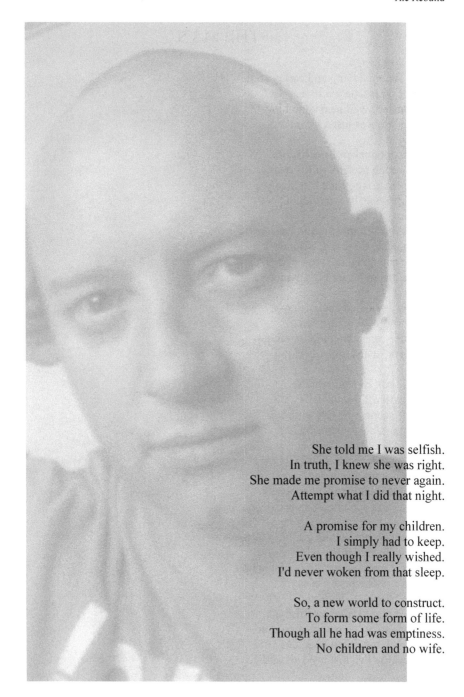

She told me I was selfish.
In truth, I knew she was right.
She made me promise to never again.
Attempt what I did that night.

A promise for my children.
I simply had to keep.
Even though I really wished.
I'd never woken from that sleep.

So, a new world to construct.
To form some form of life.
Though all he had was emptiness.
No children and no wife.

THE DISTRACTION

So, now the next phase would begin.
A new home, he would rent.
A new job would be offered.
And this was heaven sent.

An old friend would reach out to me.
"Coops, will you come and work"
"For my delivery company, please?"
Turning it down would be berserk!

Driving was my freedom.
It was like my superpower.
No day mirrored the last one.
I'd work, no matter what the hour.

Whether sticking to my daily round.
Interacting with my regular clients.
Or driving the length of the country.
To deliver a railway appliance.

It's where I found some freedom.
I loved being on the road.
Every client seemed to like me.
My joy from work just showed.

Twelve, to sixteen hours per day.
For six days every week.
I'd have done seven days but couldn't.
Closed on Sundays, what a cheek!

Though this opened opportunity.
For me to see my kids.
My youngest with me every week.
We'd 'veg out' and eat like pigs.

Collect them on a Friday.
Off to Morrisons we'd go.
To buy a pile of junk food.
And Cream Soda would overflow.

cont.

We'd sit and laugh at YouTube.
This became our routine.
Did 'Mini Coops' want to live with me?
Could anything get between.

The bond that we were building.
The impact it had made.
Upon the lives that we both lived.
Had I finally made the grade?

A father to be proud of.
The thought of that was great.
Whether we made each other happy.
Simply wasn't up for debate.

We would both laugh at the same things.
Even music taste was shared.
A guy called Jack Savoretti.
Was our favourite, we declared.

One evening, in my kitchen.
A message was sent to me.
A special friend surprised us and said.
"Jack Savoretti, you're going to see"

I'm not ashamed to admit.
That we both shed some tears.
Though these were tears of happiness.
For the first time in several years.

This was the last week of September.
The year, two thousand and nineteen.
The concert on the first day of November.
This was the happiest we'd been.

But fate would have to intervene.
Of course it would, it's me.
Happiness just never lasts.
It's a literal guarantee!

So, I'll go to the next chapter.
Where I'll tell you & insist.
Coopsie and happiness.
Just cannot coexist!

THE REBUILD!

So, this is where we move on to the next step of this journey I've been put on. Where I attempt to introduce you to, quite literally, the most amazing people I've ever encountered. It's almost doing them a disservice, calling them People. There's a reason you'll be seeing my use the term "Angels" because, to me, that's precisely what I woke up and was greeted by after 6 weeks of blackness!

This is where I hope to let you know about each person, each specialist, each department that slowly, but surely started to rebuild a man from nothing to something, and from something to someone!

It will end when you're introduced to the Occupational Therapy Department!

Intensive care, Tempest Ward, is the next step we take. I just hope I'm able to do them justice. Words will never be enough to express just how special these people are. Every person, every department went above and beyond anything I've ever encountered.

So, allow me to tentatively introduce you to Tempest. The very reason you're able to read these words!

THE GATES OF HELL DID OPEN

Excitement slowly building.
As the concert is now near.
Three weeks until we go see Jack.
But excitement would soon disappear.

After driving round the country.
Another twelve hour day.
Never in my worst nightmare.
Could happiness end this way.

A quick shower and a bite to eat.
Then get myself in bed.
Not knowing that would be my route.
Towards hell, I would tread.

I still don't know what happened.
The only thing I know.
One minute I was drifting off.
The next in an inferno.

I just remember waking up.
Being engulfed by flames.
A fleeting thought, I'm going to die.
Who'll find my charred remains?

Like those people in the movies.
Wearing fire suits.
A walking human fireball.
One of hells latest recruits.

I'm told that, after getting out.
I'd tell the firemen.
I've got to get to that concert.
To make my youngest happy again.

They said that wouldn't happen.
I told them, "no, it must".
As Hypothermia settled in.
My happiness was crushed.

cont.

"Where's the bloody Ambulance?"
I heard the firemen say.
They became more concerned.
I was going to slip away!

But Jack was all that filled my thoughts.
No pain was felt at all.
As I'd burned all my nerves away.
That's the last thing I recall.

The night of October the ninth.
In two thousand and nineteen.
The gates of hell opened as.
I created a horror scene.

Charred beyond recognition.
The ambulance arrived.
Their crew, and the firemen.
Not knowing how I survived.

Nobody should get out.
Of what I'd just endured.
The person that I used to be.
Was gone, forever obscured.

No skin left on my body.
I'll never forget the smell.
Of burning, melted, smoking flesh.
As I walked through the gates of hell.

AM I DEAD?

The title may look silly.
But it's genuine, this question.
I remember firemen.
And death being the suggestion.

Every now and then I'd hear.
"Mr Cooper, do you know"
"You had an accident, You're in Wales"
How, if I live in Cornwall, though?

Apparently a helicopter.
Was the only way.
To get me somewhere quick enough.
To save my life that day.

I'd keep hearing voices.
Though everything was black.
Was it angels talking to me?
Is that it, no way back?

Six weeks in a coma.
I'm told, two weeks and You're dead.
So how was I hearing those.
Random voices in my head?

Thirty Five percent burns can be fatal.
I had sixty six.
Add that to the coma.
There's no way they can fix.

The man so unrecognisable.
That his son did pass him by.
"Are you sure it's my dad", he said.
"And is he going to die?"

They simply couldn't answer.
As I was unresponsive.
Machines were doing my breathing.
The care required, intensive!

cont.

My twenty two year old boy.
Would have to give permission.
Whether to turn the machines off.
What a horrible decision!

Apparently a friend bent down.
And whispered in my ear.
Something funny said at work.
And a brief smile did appear.

The first time I responded.
Or, at least that's what I'm told.
Was I brain dead, no-one knew.
As I just lay there cold.

Why was I hearing voices.
When everything was black.
Is this what being dead is like?
Will my kids get their dad back?

Eventually I woke up.
But couldn't speak a note.
'Cos the tube that kept me breathing.
Was threaded down my throat.

I tried my best to make some sense.
Of what I'd woken to.
Intensive care, Tempest Ward.
That's where you are now, Stu.

People rushing everywhere.
All of this for me.
Eventually I'd discover.
It's angels that I see.

A gradual introduction.
To people who would rebuild.
A person no-one could comprehend.
Somehow, hadn't been killed.

By a fire he did not know of.
With injuries so bad.   cont.

14

That his children faced the prospect.
Of not having a dad.

For them, I had to fight on.
That's precisely what I'd do.
So next I'm going to tell you.
What I had to go through.

To give myself the best chance.
A guy who loved a fight.
I walked through hell, I cheated death.
When I should have died that night!

At least I finally knew.
As I lay there in that bed.
Couldn't talk, couldn't walk.
But no Coops, You're not dead!

A LIFE FOREVER CHANGED

Shortly after my life was saved
A lengthy rebuild would begin
Not just for my body
But also the person within

A lady came to see me
She said Helen was her name
Little did I know at the time
Life would never be the same

Whilst I could build my body up
My mind was always broken
Yet Helen was somehow fixing it
With every word she'd spoken

I spoke of things I'd previously
Never spoken before
Yet somehow this amazing lady
Could coax out even more

Tears, anger and frustration
These are things I'd never displayed
With Mindfulness for relaxation
What a difference she had made

So did she fix my broken mind?
Well yes, and more you see
Because Helen made me realise
That what matters most is me

AN ANGEL IN MY WORLD

Every now and then in life
Someone special comes along
Your heartstrings suddenly tugged
To compose the most beautiful song

Well, this person did appear to me
In my deepest hour of need
Let me suffer, she would not
Was she an angel? Yes indeed!

Heavenly sent, but she 'got me'
Knowing I just didn't want to suffer
And from the first time that she saw me
She became my safety buffer

But why did this angel do this?
Deserve it, I did not
After-all, she couldn't know
I'd lost everything I've got

Yet she changed days off to suit me
Could she really do much more?
Except almost cry when she saw me
Trying to run in the corridor

So I wish that I could find a way
For the whole world to be shown
That the angel that appeared to me
Is a name that can't be known.

This is what the hospital said.
So I simply must respect.
Data protection restricts me here.
Though, what else did I expect?

I cannot lead the life I want.
I can't say how I feel.
But, rest assured gratitude.
Is the only thing I feel.

HE KNOWS ME BETTER THAN ANYONE

After so many months in hospital
And theatre trips aplenty
A man very reliably informed me
That is was many more than twenty

The reliable man would always meet
Then greet me at the ward
Honestly, he did it so many times
Yet, not once did he ever seem bored

Always jolly and full of life
But sensitive and caring too
He could tell if you're cold, or feeling some pain
And he always knew just what to do

One day it wasn't much fun, though
As I lay there on the bed
I could see that he was ravaged with pain
And it wasn't in his head

Low and behold, next time I was there
He most certainly was not
The pain he was in had kept him away
Due to the bad belly he'd got.

Did he return me better than ever?
You bet your life he did
And I was glad, because it's been a pleasure to meet
This man, from who I never hid.

MORRISTON MUSINGS

A few words of expression
Because a Physio asked me to
It's almost as though she truly believes
I've not got enough to do

With O.T in the mornings
Then physio after that
Then afternoons for counselling
I'm a busy little prat

But six months ago, I almost died
So I shouldn't really complain
Because I'm still here after a bit of hard work
And an awful lot of pain

My life has changed forever
A long fight lies ahead
But I'll fight so I'll hopefully once again
Get to tuck my kids into bed

Hospital hasn't been too bad
They've catered for my every need
Though we did have the odd hiccup
When it comes to my daily feed

And all the staff are angels
With many I'll never forget
I've cried with them, I've laughed with them
They're some of the best people I've ever met

Stuart "Coopsie" Cooper

THANK YOU FOR A FUTURE

How can one begin to thank
People that have done so much
The doctors, surgeons, the anaesthetic team
They've changed me with every touch

They started by keeping me breathing
When I arrived in quite a state
From what I've heard, it wouldn't be long
Before it was too late

I was burnt beyond recognition
My son even passed me by
If it wasn't for those I've mentioned
It was probable that I'd die

But the doctors pulled me through it
Then it was the anaesthetists turn
To prepare me for the surgeons
To rebuild me burn by burn

Over thirty visits to theatre
Well at least that's what I'm told
But that theatre team has given me chance
To gracefully grow old

Again, how do I thank them
For the life they've given me
For them I'll carry gratitude
For all eternity

WHO KNEW ANGELS ARE REAL

The discovery happened months ago
Holding to life by a thread
A helicopter would rush me to Wales
Not knowing what fate lay ahead
Keeping little old me alive
Started on Tempest Ward
They tell me survival was touch and go
One mistake, they couldn't afford
Angels started to show them selves
Little was I to know
Lay there in a comatosed state
Weeks would come and go
Heaven knows how they saved me
Only they could say
Hearing a knock upon deaths door
Entered angels on that day
Love for them will stay with me
Proud of them I feel
Everyone on Tempest Ward
Did show that angels are real

WORDS JUST AREN'T ENOUGH

I've taken on the impossible task
Of somehow trying to thank
A man whom if it wasn't for him
Six foot down I would be sank

October the ninth, two thousand and nineteen
He took me under his care
At Morriston Hospital, in Tempest Ward
With me not even knowing I was there

Destroyed by an explosion, engulfed by fire
It's no exaggeration to say
Were it not for the skills of this wonderful man
I would not be here today

Through countless routines in theatre
He and his team would undertake
The rebuilding of a broken man
Who'd be grateful each time he'd awake

Thanks to him my children
Still have a dad to love
If I believed in religion
I'd swear he was sent from above

But there is sadly nothing
A man such as me could do
To ever repay all that he's done
But thank you for pulling me through!

THE TRANSITION

So, after the wonderful people in Tempest Ward somehow saved the life of the man who was given little chance of survival. The time came to be moved from Intensive Care, to the new, scary surroundings that would be known as Powys Ward.

I was wheeled down to the ward a couple of weeks prior to actually being moved from Intensive Care to Powys Ward, to be introduced to the people that would end up supporting and rebuilding me for the next 7 months.

Room D would no longer be known as "Room D". For the next 7 months, "Room D" simply became "Stuarts Room". It would become not just my safe haven, but also the place where "The Angels" in Powys Ward, along with the odd visit from the special people from Tempest Ward, would come to unload, take a breather and Stuart Cooper became the man that would somehow make these amazing people feel better each time they entered my room!

You are about to be introduced to the phenomenal people that would fill the next 7 months of this existence I'd been thrust into. There will never be enough words to do these people justice!

However, every word You're about to read was wonderfully received by each person written about. There really isn't anything that can compare to seeing people react with genuine emotion, from words You've written about them.

Sadly, The Hospital has requested me to not name the wonderful nurses, surgeons, Anaesthetists, OT's, physios etc etc.

However, please allow me to walk you from the beautiful people in Tempest Ward, to their fellow angels in Powys Ward.

A HIDDEN GEM

It's hard for me to put into words
A description of this young lady
So quiet, receptive and genuine
There's nothing deceitful or shady

She cares because she's caring
She listens to all you say
No matter what you ask of her
It'll be done, whether night or day

There's just so much potential
For this girl, the sky's the limit
The nursing world is hers to take
If she just grasps what's within it

Already, in her young life
She's achieved such a great deal
But I know she could have so much more
It's just the way I feel

She could easily advance to run a ward
As she possesses all it takes
I'm not the only one who sees this
So why can't she, for goodness sakes?

We only want what's best for her
I wish she'd listen to me and them
The nurse I refer to, I cannot name
Powys Wards hidden gem

A STRANGER MADE A DIFFERENCE

She came to me from Pembroke
When the wards got changed around
I didn't know what to expect
But she was really pretty sound

To be fair, they all seemed okay
But this girl just stood out
Because she just took time for me
Which is what it's all about

She'd come to my room and listen
She'd give me good advice
It was very easy for me to tell
That she was simply very nice

We hit it off quite quickly
A fair few laughs we'd share
But who's this lady I speak of?
A lady born to care.

When I'm down, she seems to notice
And she tries to make me smile
Although that's not easy with me
She succeeds once in a while

I hope she knows I'm grateful
As a nurse, she's a special one
And with teared up eyes, I must admit
I'll miss her when I'm gone.

CHANGE IS SUCH A SHAME

A lady came into my life
While I was going through hell
My head is what she came to fix
And open up my heart, to tell

No way was this task easy
No way could it be done
As this man is no open book
From help, he'd run for fun!

But slowly, and with patience
She began to pick the lock
Bringing together my feelings and thoughts
Like a shepherd would gather his flock

Emotions started pouring out
This had never happened before
Had she achieved the unachievable
And unlocked the unlockable door?

In truth, she did much more than that
She built a whole new man
Before, he asked if he could matter
She made him see he can

So, as she moves to pastures new
I wish her all the best
A lady that helped me see myself
She passed the unpassable test!

IMPOSSIBLE NOT TO LOVE

Every now and then in life
Someone comes along
The type of person for whom you could
Compose a special song

They just have something about them
But they don't seek attention
When it comes to personality traits
There are far too many to mention

Well, I've come across such a person
Since I've been in Powys Ward
And whenever she's around you
It's impossible to be bored

I've tried my best to hate her
But it's impossible to do
You just can't help but crack up
If she simply looks at you

She's full of fun and mischief
I want to scream her name
I swear to you I've never met
Anyone quite the same

So, how can I describe this gift?
Well, she's an angel from above
With more than a hint of devilment
And impossible not to love!

LATE TO THE PARTY BUT I'M GLAD SHE CAME

I met this nurse after the rest
As she was on maternity leave
I knew instantly, after one brief chat
That, in her I could believe

Her knowledge oozed from every word
And the care was genuine, too
She made me know not to worry
Because she knew just what to do

She makes her job look easy
No matter how bust things get
Here, there and everywhere
One of the best that I've seen yet

Whether day or night shift
Not a difference does it make
But if your wounds could do with creaming
Approach with caution for your own sake

The girl is obsessed with picking
She simply doesn't care
She'll take your scabs, she'll take your skin
There'll be bugger all left there

A truly wonderful lady
Who I'm tuly blessed to know
A future sister, or ward manager
That's how far she can go!

MEET HIM AT YOUR PERIL

I'm not sure I've ever met
A person so random and weird
Fishing around for compliments
About his stupid bloody beard

But trust me, that is nothing
Compared to what he'll do
When you think You're used to him
Trust me, he'll shock you

He'll give you a false sense of security
He'll make you think he has a heart
Then he'll think nothing of calmly turning around
And letting rip the loudest fart

He does it without warning
He does it without care
And as for what goes on in his head
Sigmund Freud wouldn't even go there

Yet despite all this, I must admit
And it comes through gritted teeth
The place just wouldn't be the same
Without the weirdo that's comic relief.

MORE IMPORTANT THAN YOU THINK

As I sit here in my little chair
In the corner of my room
I watch people through my window
As here and there, they zoom

But through the frantic relentlessness
One person, static she stays
Calm, composed and beautiful
I could look at her for days

She sits behind her counter
All quiet and unassuming
But thanks to her organisation skills
The Powys Ward traffic is booming

Sorting files, or taking calls
Directing people where to go
I watch her and can't help but think
Is there anything she doesn't know?

She'll even pass my hospital gown
Or make me a cup of tea
Nothing's too much trouble for her
She's as kind as a person could be

So, it surely can't be doubted
That she makes Powys Ward tick
And I hope the staff all realise
Their receptionist is magic!

MORE THAN JUST A NURSE

I was moved from Tempest Ward
No more intensive care
I was apprehensive about the new ward
Not knowing what lay ahead there

As I got to my room a nurse asked
"Hi ya, how are you?"
I said, "Hi, I'm living the dream!"
She said, "Hey, you can't say that, I do!"

From that point on we hit it off
Much banter we would share
But the thing that I'll remember the most
Is the extraordinary level of care

She became more than a nurse to me
As we realised we're the same
The music we liked, the thoughts we shared
She made me glad I came

An extremely special person
I was growing to know
She guided me physically and mentally
Until the time came to go

No words could ever thank her
No words would ever do
So, with certainty I say to this Angel
I'll never forget you!

OUR BIT OF CRAZY

Fiery, firm but friendly
That's this nurse to a tee
But if she wakes me up again
She'll see the worst of me

She's louder than a foghorn
Her laugh could wake the dead
If you ask her, even she'd agree
She's not right in the head

But please don't let that fool you
She's damn good at her job
The girl gets through just as much work
As her ever flapping gob

I don't know how she finds the time
To work between the words
They should pay her more, then use her laugh
To scare away the birds

I'll not bring up her twerking
As she showed us all one night
Or pressing herself against my window
Stevie Wonder would find that a sight

Thankfully this nurse knows me
And that these words are all in jest
Because when it comes to people in Powys
She's up there with the best!

POTENTIALLY AMAZING

So quiet and unassuming
So chilled, relaxed and calm
A lovely girl that you just know
Would never cause you harm

It's easy to see she loves her job
No matter what the task
And when it comes to helping you
Nothing's too much to ask!

She'll do all that she can to help
No matter what your need
With a wisdom far beyond her years
A very fine nurse indeed

Ask for your meds early
She'll see that it gets done
But please don't think she's all just work
She's also loads of fun

I've often heard her giggling with
The girls as they share a joke
And I say with all sincerity
I mean every word I've spoke

A future that's so full of promise
A nurse that's full of care
Sweetheart it's now down to you
You can truly go anywhere!

SHE'S UNIQUE

Take a walk on the wild side
My parents said to me
If they could look into my future
They'd see it's as wild as can be

Though nothing would prepare me
For what the future would bring
Where a hospital stay introduced me
To one hell of a unique thing

You've heard of the film and musical
The classic, A Star Is Born.
Well, let me tell you, when I'm gone
I genuinely will mourn.

A talkative and confident girl
A voice so loud and clear
She's standing next to me talking now
I'll still hear her next year

Whether morning, or a night shift
What you see is what you get
If there's another person like her
I haven't met them yet!

But in the end I'm grateful
She's helped nurse me back to health
And I hope our Siobhans future
Is filled with happiness, joy and wealth

SMALL GIRL, BIG HEART

The time is coming to say farewell
But it's time for thank you's, too
It's not everyone's cup of tea
To me, it's the right thing to do

You see, since I've been in Powys Ward
Many nurses I have seen
Some have been good, others not so much
And some, sort of in between

But the odd one has stood out to me
These words refer to one
But you just can't help but know
You'll miss her when you're gone

She's not the sort that shouts or screams
Attention, she doesn't crave
The sort of girl that you could just
Never see misbehave

I'm so grateful for all she's done
While I've been on the mend
So, special thanks to a special nurse
For being my Powys friend!

THE GIFT THAT JUST KEEPS GIVING

How can I describe this one
with just a page of words?
So special that, if she was a meal
Stuff seconds, I'd have thirds!

To look at, she's just lovely
A sight worth waiting for
She's great just to watch doing something
Because you never know what's in store

Sometimes you sit and wonder
What the hell is she doing now?
Yet the task ends up completed
And even she doesn't know how

The skills she has are endless
I'm honest, so that must be said
While I was here, she even managed
To fix a broken bed

She makes a lovely cuppa
But more importantly, she's fun
Don't ask her for porridge, though
It's hotter than the sun!

There's not much more that I can say
She's a carer for a living
So, thank you just for being you
The gift that just keeps giving!

THERE ARE NO FAULTS

Six and a half long months ago
There was a nurse I'd get to meet
And like many other nurses
She was attentive, kind and sweet

But there were other sides to her
Which I'd learn the more we talked
And people may just understand
If in her shoes they'd walked

She's such an attractive young lady
But see it, she does not
Self appraisal is not her thing
She's never seen what she's got

She told me that to make me see
When we chatted late one night
That I shouldn't worry about my looks
As it's not about what is in sight

If only she'd listen to her own words
But also hear mine, too
Because to look at, she's just lovely
She must believe that's true!

So, who's this nurse I got to meet
Though I can't name who I'm on about
I think the whole world needs to know
She's stunning inside and out!

YEAH, THEY WERE ALRIGHT

Deep into my hospital stay
The Corona Virus came
From that day onwards Powys Ward
Would never be the same

The merger would come with the Ward above
New nurses and domestics would appear
What would they be like? Would they fit in?
The answer would soon be clear

I thought our ward was broken
The atmosphere had changed
Some Powys staff were sent elsewhere
They were hijacked, stolen, estranged!

But the new staff slowly settled
And it turns out they were nice
They soon mixed in with Powys staff
And some would listen and give advice

I'll admit some women were stunning
As people, not just to the eye
It's a tearful ending for this monster
So, thank You Pembroke, Goodbye

*Please note the following page has a picture of Stuart's burns to the head!

YOU WOULDN'T KNOW IF I DIDN'T TELL YOU

She welcomed me to Powys Ward
Before I was even admitted
When they brought me down from Tempest
And I instantly knew she was committed

To making patients comfortable
In the ward she'd run with care
I knew I had little to worry about
When I would make the move down there

Well, "there" soon became "here"
And "here" is where I'll stay
For many, many, many months
But I'd be cared for every day

This is largely down to how
The ward is ultimately run
The girls have tasks, and must do jobs
But have freedom for a little fun

Powys is a truly special ward
You can take that as gospel from me
So, I'll say without a shadow of doubt
The sister is as good as can be!

YOU'D STRUGGLE TO FIND BETTER

Authoritative and stern looking
But don't be fooled by looks
Kind, gentle and empathetic
One of the best on Powys' books

Yes, she's very matter of fact
And she says things as they are
But surely truth is what you want
After battling to get this far

When it comes to doing her job
She's very bloody good
She made the biggest impression on me
As the tears of mine did flood

Because of how ugly I've become
Down in front of me she got
And told me in no uncertain terms
Looks matter not one jot!

Then she told me I'm not ugly
I could tell she understood
That I simply needed picking up
Like I said, she's bloody good!

Whether dressing my head late at night
Or waking me on a winter's morn.
When this Angel came into the world
A gift to nursing was born

SORRY IF I MISSED YOU

It just happened so quickly
I honestly had no idea
The sister just appeared to say
"Tomorrow, you may not be here"

Talk about unexpected
A bolt out of the blue
I was just left sat there thinking
Coops, this could only happen to you!

It was only a few short weeks ago
I was reassured, I'd be discharged home
Then possibly, with less than a days notice
Words were forgotten, I was alone

To face a world of strangers
People I'd never met
People I don't even want to meet
Well, at least not yet!

But as usual I'm powerless
With what happens in my life
A life that would be empty
If bad wasn't always rife

So, if I left without you knowing
Or without saying goodbye
Please know, you have my word on this
I'll remember you until I die

ALLOW ME TO INTRODUCE PHYSIO 1

One day during torture session
Or 'Physio' as it's known
Halfway through getting my arms stretched off
A new face would be shown

A student within the physio team
She settles real quick
But while exercising I worried that
My appearance would make her sick

But like a world class hurdler
She took things in her stride
I can't say how her mentors feel
But she's sure filled me with pride

So quiet and unassuming
You'd barely know she's there
'til she encourages, or says "Well done"
She's filled with genuine care

Then sessions move to outside
And she becomes a different girl
Quite frankly, she's just fearless
She'll give anything a whirl

So pretty on the outside
Yet more beautiful within
No matter what she does in life
I've no doubt that she'll win!

LADIES AND GENTLEMEN, PHYSIO 2

One day she sprung from nowhere
A completely brand new face
She was rather pleasing to the eye
This girl would be my race

She'll bond with you dead quickly
She'll make you feel at ease
She's approachable and friendly
She does all she can to please

Well, that's unless she's competing
Then she'll please you not one bit
As long as she beats you somehow
She couldn't give a , umm, damn

This lady's greatest quality
Is the confidence she exudes
And her cracking sense of humour
She'll keep you well amused

But don't be fooled by her humour
She really knows her stuff
She knows when to do things gently
And when to do them rough

Have a question? She'll answer it clearly
She'll explain it really well
I knew from the moment I met her
She'll go far, I could just tell.

MEET FOOTBALL PHYSIO

My physio sessions had just began
A new face did appear
Tall, long legs and blonde on top
I thought "lookee what we have here"

Then I found out she played football
I mean, could this get any better?
A pretty, leggy blonde football player
A genuine standard setter.

But, unlike the stereotypical blonde
There was substance within the shell
Her intelligence left me nothing to fear
I was safe here, I could tell

She gave me an easy feeling
My mind was put at ease
So, if Laura tried to push me
I'd do all I could to please

Respect, it is a two way street
Where each must give and take
Could I do what she asked of me?
I'd have to, for my own sake

How far in her field can this girl go?
It's impossible to measure
But I can say with utmost sincerity
Young lady, it's been a pleasure

STERN, STRONG, SPECIAL

I woke from a two month coma
Machines breathing for me, unable to talk
In fact, although not known to me
I couldn't even walk

A metaphorical mountain
Was the climb I had ahead
Which surely wasn't possible
Each step filled with utter dread

But a lady would appear to me
"Hi, I'm Your physio" She said
She was the physiotherapist
Who would get me out of bed

Although my body was broken
Deterred, this angel was not
I quickly came to realise
I'd have to give her all I've got

To have any chance of recovery
Her strictness was what I required
Never taking "No" for an answer
Even though in pain or tired

She pushes me to my limit
At times we went beyond
She made that metaphorical mountain
Seem like the flattest pond

And now I'm fit for discharge
With my butt well and truly spanked
If I'm ever to come back here
It'll be her that's first to be thanked!

THE SPICE GIRLS

Remember in the nineties
From nowhere they appeared
Hit after hit, and number ones
A phenomenon was reared

But it couldn't last forever
New professions they would seek
Little did I realise then
I'd get to see them every week

They each claimed new identities
And left for pastures new
They'd land at Morrison Hospital
To be physios for me and you

The first I met was Scary Spice
I cannot say her name
Who, despite the new identity
Is still scary, all the same

Sporty became Football Physio
She's bright, nobody's fool
Yet she lets herself down badly
By supporting Liverpool

Then we come to Posh Spice
She's posh, "Oh look I ski"
"I also cheat at card games"
Oh shit! She's a female me!

Last up we have Baby Spice
One of the nicest girls you'll meet
She's pretty and funny, with a beautiful soul
But owns a stranger's feet!

THE TORTURE TEAM

The physio girls have asked me
And I just can't believe this
To put together a poem
In which I take the piss

I'll start it off with the big boss
She's the leader of the pack
She'll push you, inflict a world of pain
She's an addict and pain is her crack

Then of course there's Football Girl
The equivalent of Sporty Spice
Blonde on top and inside too
And likes to pretend she's nice

Next up we have Physio 2
All innocent and sweet
You'll laugh if you watch her play football
It's like she's borrowed someone else's feet

Finally we come to one
For whom there are no words
To describe just how annoying she is
She's constipation in a life of turds

RIDICULOUSLY RANDOM

These next couple of chapters are, well, Ridiculously Random. Allow me to explain, please!

You see, after the wonderful physio team in Morriston decided it was time to start trying to use my hands again, giving me dexterity exercises and strengthening exercises. They decided it was also time to see if I could once again learn to hold a pen and carry out some simple writing tasks.

This is where my stupid ego ended up biting me on my charred behind. Even while at School and college, I despised anything academical. But I particularly despised writing. However, I'm that guy who CAN'T say no to anyone who's tried to help him, and the crafty physio girls knew this. The sneaky little so & so's!

I'll explain this next chapter as well as I possibly can. But, be warned. Random doesn't come close to covering what you're about to read.

Those physio girls asked me to write something overnight and take it to my session the next day. Oh how great, homework. Being the adult 45 year old man that I was, I obviously had a tantrum, rolled my eyes at them and simply said "fine", and off they went, leaving me with my orders for the evening.

Great, writing when I hate writing. Writing when I can't hold a pen. Writing when I have absolutely no imagination whatsoever. What the heck was I supposed to write about? Ironically, my mind instantly went back to my school days. Days when I would pay next to no attention to what the teacher was saying, because I was too busy writing silly little limericks about the teacher & passing them around the classroom for cheap laughs.

So, my mind was made up for me. I'd write a silly little poem for the physio girls. Or, at least that's what I thought!. I may be wrong here, but I THINK the poem was "Who knew Angels Are Real", which was in The Tempest Ward Chapter earlier in the book. But I digress!

I decided my homework would be a little poem about what I'd experienced since waking from the coma. The care given to me & the beautiful people who'd provided it. Little did I know what my 20 minute doodle would result in.

As the next day began, I made my way to the physio department and, like a stroppy teenager, threw my doodle on the table and said "here's your flipping homework", and stropped off into the gym to give myself a beasting on the multigym. That beasting didn't last long! Next thing I see, is a bunch of tearful physios and nurses stood in front of me. Turns out, this doodle made quite the impact. But how? It is just words, not hard to do.

I was asked, "How did you come up with that overnight?". And with me being in the stroppy, dismissive mood that I was in that morning, simply responded with. "I didn't, I came up with it in about 20 minutes and couldn't be bothered to do any more".

And then that ego of mine that I mentioned, REALLY kicked in. As did my unfiltered mouth, by saying to those physios & nurses. "It wasn't exactly difficult, I can write stupid poetry about absolutely anything!".

My dad always told me this mouth of mine would get me into trouble one day and, as always, he was absolutely spot on. Those words I uttered to those physios & nurses, were like dangling a piece of Prime Cut Steak in front of a pride of lions. "Oh really?" they said!

"Yep, ANYTHING", I responded. Me and my big mouth had gone and done it again. My words became a challenge for the physio girls. The gauntlet was well and truly thrown down, as I literally saw all of their eyes simultaneously light up & a wry smile appear on each of their faces.

The title of this little explanation really does say it all. Because, "Ridiculously Random" is what You're about to read. The physios decided, each day, each session would require me to bring yet more poems. Poems about anything and everything random that they could possibly come up with. In an attempt to catch me out. Mr Big Mouth here, who said "Yep, ANYTHING!"

I'll learn to keep this ever flapping bracket on the front of my face shut one day. But for now, I'll leave it up to you to decide whether they caught me out. They admitted they tried and failed (I'm not at all smug about that, honest!). So, please read on and embrace the randomness that awaits!

FOOD

Food is something we all need
For us to stay alive
Three meals a day is what they say
But I could happily eat five

Whether Carnivore, Vegan or Veggie
We all have a favourite meal
Veggies like Tofu, and I like bacon
So, squeal piggie, squeal!

Stew is great for Winter
It warms you from within
But let's not mention hospital food
It's only good for the fu*@ing bin!

FOOTBALL

How do you write a poem
About a sport that means so much
It's more than simply just a game
It's about control, technique and touch

You either love it or you hate it
There is no in-between
It's a love that cannot be described
A love that can only be seen

Whether crunching into tackles
Or sprinting down the wing
Skinning someone with a Cruyff turn
It's such a beautiful thing

There is one part that can't be described
The art of scoring a goal
The feeling within, it's pure elation
It's joy food for your soul

Not everybody likes it, though
But if you don't, you're lame
Because there's nothing like the passion
Within Football, The Beautiful Game

GARDENING

The sun is out, the air is fresh
That's fulfilled many needs
Is it time to step outside
And rid the garden of weeds

You start with good intentions
You get the wellies out
You get your gloves and secateurs
Then give the dog a shout

Your first task is the flower beds
Though they don't need that much done
But you're getting in the groove now
This gardening lark is fun!

The dog is having a great time
She loves sharing your fun
Messing around with a squeaky toy
Or crashing in the sun

You may not have green fingers
And that summer soil may harden
But there's not much that's more pleasing
Than some time out in the garden

GOLF

A sport that's a bit like Marmite
A real love or hate thing
It takes years of practice and patience
To find the perfect swing

It's created some sporting legends
Ballesteros, Faldo and Woods
True icons in a sport that's art
They always produced the goods

I've seen golf described as "a waste of a walk"
To some, I guess this is true
Those people should try to give it a go
Because it's really not easy to do

A good swing is a thing of beauty
One motion of control and grace
But you must relax and take your time
Because golf is not a race

I played golf for years
My dad's present to his son
And he used that time to teach me
To relax and have some fun

HOLIDAYS

Everybody needs one
At some point in their life
Whether alone, or with the family
Or a short break with the wife

Youngsters hit the club scene
They large it in Ibiza
The more mature folk head elsewhere
With scenery as their favourite feature

Families like a package deal
With a hotel, pool and beach
Germans like a sunbed
They reserve at least 3 each

Some people don't even go abroad
They have what's called a "Stay-cation"
After-all there's some stunning places
In our tiny island nation

Whether Cornwall, Wales or Scotland
There's plenty to enjoy
Stunning scenery, and friendly folk
Await every girl and boy

We work hard for a living
We do the best we can
So, there's nothing wrong with taking time off
To relax, or top up your tan.

MUSICALS

Tim Rice and Andrew Lloyd-Webber
Are giants of the industry
They've probably written, composed and created
Any musical you'll ever see

There's Phantom of the Opera
Then Evita, and Cats, too.
They've brought us many classics
It's amazing what they do

There's also Cameron Mackintosh
Who brought us the best of all
The spell-binding Les Miserables
Where the repressed will fight, not fall

Everyone should go to London
To visit The West End
And broaden their cultural horizons
A broken soul, it will surely mend

So, whether it's We Will Rock You
Or the beautiful Miss Saigon
I hope that musicals never end
'cos as they say, The Show Must Go On!

NATURE

Nature's all around us
When we step outside
Whether the sweet song of a bird
Or the sun shining on a bride

It provides us all with beauty
Which some people fail to see
They hunt animals for pleasure
Which is sickening to me!

Nature gives us weather
Such an unpredictable thing
One minute you're basking in sunshine
The next it's thunder and lightening

The pain of being in a hail storm
A shelter is where to go
And then we do the opposite
When we have a sprinkling of snow

It could be animal, weather or surroundings
Or the clouds in the sky above
It should be something that we all embrace
It should be something we all love!

Stuart "Coopsie" Cooper

WEATHER

Rain, hail, snow or storm
It's hard to know what it'll do
The only thing we know for sure
Is there's no escape for me or you

But it can be a thing of beauty
Just watch a lightning storm
It truly is a beautiful thing
Watching Mother Nature perform

The power of a cyclone
As it twists its path of destruction
Flattening homes and picking up cars
It's awesome to watch one function

The rain can bring us flooding
The sun can bring us drought
Displaying power that's hard to behold
Is what the weather is all about

A VERY SPECIAL TEAM

A team of fine young ladies
Selfless to a point
Would patiently assess me
Joint by little joint

Their task, it wasn't easy
My body buckled and burned
They'd surely have to call upon
Everything they'd ever learned

But through countless hours of creaming
Pressure garments, splints and gloves
I could see that each and every girl
Was doing a job she loves

Yet those Occupational Therapists
Would still do so much more
As they try their best to get me
The keys to my new front door

They prepared me for my discharge
Forever grateful I will be
So thanks to each and everyone
The wonderful ladies from O.T.

MEANDERISH

Firstly, yes. I totally made up a word because it fits my agenda & perfectly describes what this next chapter entails.
There's appreciation for, and towards others.
There's an attempt to describe the joys of parenthood.
There's questions within questions.
There's an attempt to describe my first social outing.

There's almost no direction this next little chapter doesn't take. The very definition of the word "Meander," is "A Journey that has no particular direction".

Yep, that's certainly the next chapter. There really is no other way for me to describe it. So, follow me for a Meander down the chapter that is the most Meanderish of all

HONESTY IN IT'S PUREST FORM

Some people write for a living
In broadsheets, magazines and papers
But face it, most of what we read
Is written by liars and fakers

These people are paid a fortune
To be soulless corporate hacks
Demonstrating a blatant disregard
For little things we call "Facts"

This is where I come in
To express my pure disdain
For people who use the written word
To lie time and again

A truly passionate writer
Who writes from deep within
Could never sell their soul like that
They'd judge it as a sin

It's easy to write nonsense
Toddlers do it all the time
And they probably have more integrity
Than those hacks committing written crime

If it's honesty you want
And you'd like to be the norm
Pen yourself some poetry
'cos that's honesty in its purest form!

LOSING THE PLOT

Sitting in Derriford staring at a wall
As there's nothing else to do
It's the 21st bloody Century
But in here it's 1902

How can I have no Wi-Fi
When reception's just 10 feet away
It's doing my fucking head in
My patience gets tested each day

I'm writing bloody poetry
That's how bad it's got
Swear words running through my head
I've lost the fucking plot

I cannot watch the TV
As Derriford doesn't provide
That, or even radio
If I had tear ducts I'd have cried

Reset the God damn router
At least give it a go
Or someone's gonna get murdered
And it'll be your fault, you know!

TAKING THINGS FOR GRANTED

It's very easy in this life
To not realise what we've got
Until something awful comes along
To strip you of the lot

Whether breakdown in relationship
Or an accident so tragic
It singlehandedly decimates
All that makes life magic

The bond formed with a loved one
Perhaps the hardest thing to lose
Even after years have passed
Your hears still bares the bruise

And then we have possessions
The treasured things we keep
Could be ruined in a fire or flood
Or stolen while we sleep

Then there's physical fitness
Which can be taken in an instant
Especially if you're like me
With good luck being non-existent

So, cherish all within your world
Because life just ain't enchanted
And from experience I can tell you
Don't take anything for granted

THE GREATEST GIFT OF ALL

Gifts can come in many forms
And most are gratefully received
You watch with dread as they open yours
And when they like it, you're relieved

But there's one gift that trumps them all
It doesn't come under a tree
You'll want to keep it your whole life
It could come to you, as it has to me

It's the gift that keeps on giving
But it takes a fair bit, too
It's a gift that's sent to test us
But bring out the best in you!

You'll treasure it immediately
You'll be grateful this gift is yours
And the longer that you have it
You'll do nothing but open doors

I'm speaking metaphorically
Not in the literal sense
To look after this gift properly
Will make you feel immense

So, do not take it lightly
As it's simply just too good
To be truly blessed is to receive
The gift of Parenthood

TOTAL TREPIDATION

A man admitting being scared
Is not an easy thing
But for the first time in three years
I faced a social gathering

Invited by a carer who
I cannot say "No" to
Because she's been so good to me
This is something I must do

It won't just be her there, though
Friends and family tagging along
What if they don't like me?
This could all go so wrong!

I've never met these people
Though they've all heard about me
But what will their reaction be?
When this monster, they do see!

The first thing I had to face
Was being picked up from home
In a car with people I don't know
Looking like a melted, deformed gnome

Shaking like a shitting dog
I was offered the front seat
Introduced to her partner and friend
They met this battered lump of meat

As we drove down to the club
We chatted and broke the ice
These people didn't react to me
Quite simply, they were nice!

Her partner did the driving
He was introduced as "Luke"
I'd heard so much about him
But I'm just glad he didn't puke

cont.

When he laid his eyes upon me
He didn't seem to care
You could just tell, he's good people
In the modern world, that's rare!

So friendly and accepting
We even had a laugh
Taking the piss out of my carers friend
And this amazing member of staff

The friend, her name was Ellie
Blonde in every sense
Honestly, some stuff she said
was truly bloody dense.

"Do we have prawns in Cornwall?"
As if any of us would know
But from that very moment
I knew how this evening would go.

But, because of Ellie's question
Google actually says
Prawns are indeed fished down here
In Cornish estuaries and bays

Using lightweight plastic prawn pots
With a unique design
So undersized ones can be set back
To be caught another time

We pull up at the venue
Where this evening will be hosted
The first time people see
This man that's slightly toasted

An old friend was first to greet me
The hostess known as Sue
She hugged me and whispered in my ear
"My angel, You're still Stu!"

She could feel me shaking
The fear I couldn't hide   cont.

But more hugs were soon to come my way
As we all gathered outside

My carer then proceeded
To let me meet her mother
"This is Mum", who hugged me tight
I said "Mother, let's have another"

So we did, and it was lovely
I learned her name was Kerry
Another little hidden gem
Was she nice? Yes, very!

The next one that was introduced
Was the rather lovely Suzie
Who also got a Coopsie hug
And spent the evening next to me

When I say she's rather lovely
As a person, she's the best
I have to say that because
My carer thinks I'm a pest

But I just like good people
I could tell Suzie was one
Yes, she's pleasing on the eye
But it's now time to move on

As there's still one more person
That I was yet to meet
The rather crazy Kirsty
She doesn't do discrete

A tiny bundle of nuttyness
But as the drinks started to flow
I chuckled, thinking to myself
"Oh shit, here we go!"

On Kirsty there's no filter
The human equivalent of clogs
Shoes that simply make no sense
She's as mad as a box of frogs

cont.

This little group of people
Accepted me for me
They looked beneath this mound of scars
It was the person inside they see

The carers name, I'm yet to say
Who can manipulate this melted fella
Is the really rather special
Young lady known as Ella

It's for her that I did this
As I said, I can't say "No"
To one who's done so much for me
I simply had to go!

I faced my fears that evening
And met some beautiful people
My racing heart could probably be heard
From the top of the highest steeple

The Total Trepidation I felt
They didn't look down their noses
At the monster that was literally
A thorn surrounded by roses

So, Kirsty, Kerry and Ellie
Suzie, Luke and Ella
Thank you all for making me fit
Like the shoe from Cinderella

WHAT CAN WITHSTAND TIME?

One thing we take for granted
In this existence that we share
Has been around since the dawn of man
And it's happened everywhere

It started in its crudest form
Just rocks and bits of wood
Even then, to those that did it
It sounded pretty good

Like all else on this planet
Slowly it evolved
And thanks to it, hearts got fixed
And many problems solved

The power of this platform
Is crazily enticing
Around the globe, soul after soul
Through which it would keep slicing

I guarantee it's got yours
And all your family, too
Generation after generation
It's what it's meant to do

So, what is this phenomenon
That I've described in rhyme
Well, of course, my friends it's music
That's withstood the test of time

Martin, Sally & Louise

Photos taken by Helen Owen

This wonderful artwork created by Suzanne Phillips and was presented to the Hospital ward that I was taken care of.

Stuart also had his work published the Penny Authors anthology

"Book of Lived, v7"

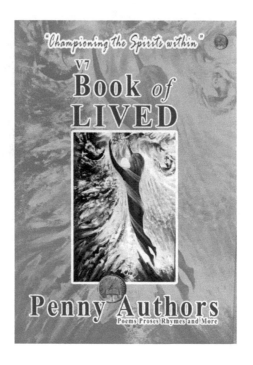

In his debut he was honoured with publishing seven of his poems, usually 4 are maximum.

It is good to see his positive progression to having his own book published.

For more information about Stuart and Penny Authors – you can check out his bio page.

https://www.pennyauthors.org.uk/poets/stuart-coopsie-cooper

MAPublisher Catalogue

ISBN/Titles /Image/Author		
Anthology One By Penny Authors	Father to child By Mayar Akash	Lit from within By Ruth Lewarne
Anthology Two By Penny Authors	River of Life By Mayar Akash	V6 Book of Lived By Penny Authors
V3 Book of Lived By Penny Authors	The Halloweeen Poem By Zainab Khan	Consciousness By Mustak Ahmed Mustafa
V4 Book of Lived By Penny Authors	Delirious By Liam Newton	V7 Book of lived By Penny Authors
V5 Book of Lived By Penny Authors	Eyewithin By Mayar Akash	Res Burman's Poetry V1 By Res J. F. Burman
When You Look Back By Rashma Mehta	Behind the tears By Rashma Mehta	The Departure Lounge By Tyrone M Warren

Cry For Help By Bhupendra M. Gandhi	Cornish Poets By Penny Authors	She Poetry By Penny Authors
My Life Book 1 By Mayar Akash	V8 Book of Lived By Penny Authors	He Poetry By Penny Authors
My Life Book 2 By Mayar Akash	Res Burman's Poety V2 By Res J. F. Burman	Surviving through Art By Jeremy J Lovelady
Angel Eyez By Rashma Mehta	The Shipwreck of my Past By Robert Cardwell-Spencer	Res Burman's Poetry V3 By Res J. F. Burman
My Dream World By Rashma Mehta	Time and tide By Rob Kersley